A New True Book

THE APACHE

By Patricia McKissack

CHILDRENS PRESS ®

CHICAGO

Apache brave at modern
Indian celebration

Library of Congress Cataloging in Publication Data

McKissack, Pat, 1944-
  The Apache.

  (A New true book)
  Includes index.
  Summary: Describes the history, customs, religion,
government, homes, and day-to-day life of the Apache
people of the Southwest.
  1. Apache Indians—Juvenile literature. [1. Apache
Indians. 2. Indians of North America] I. Title.
E99.A6M43 1984   970.004'97   84-7803
ISBN 0-516-01925-2   AACR2

TABLE OF CONTENTS

The Apachu. . . 5

The Apache Tribes. . . 7

Apache Women and Men. . . 11

Apache Marriage, Laws, and
   Customs. . . 14

Apache Leaders. . . 17

Religious Beliefs and
   Superstitions. . . 19

Growing Up Apache. . . 24

Gathering, Hunting, and
   Raiding. . . 32

The Apache Warriors and
   Wars. . . 37

The Apache Today. . . 44

Words You Should Know. . . 46

Index. . . 47

Apache girls model traditional clothes.

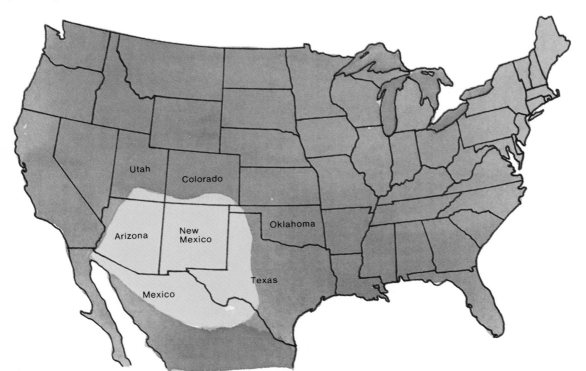

THE APACHU

The Hohokam and the Anasazi were the first people to live in the Southwest. Later the Zuni, the Papago, the Hopi, and the Pueblo came. They were farmers.

Then hunters from Canada began to move south in search of food. By the 1400s they claimed all the land that is now northern Mexico, Arizona, New Mexico, western

Bonito, a White Mountain Apache (left), and Chief San Juan and these Mescalero Apaches (right) were photographed about 1883.

Texas, and parts of Utah, Colorado, and Oklahoma.

The Zuni Indians called these newcomers Apachu ("the enemy").

The Apache were not farmers or herdsmen. They were hunters and warriors.

THE APACHE TRIBES

The Apache called themselves Tinde ("the people").

The Apache tribe can be divided into seven groups: the Navajo, Chiricahua, Lipan, Western Apache, Mescalero, Jicarilla, and Kiowa-Apache. (The Navajo later separated from the Apache. They became an independent tribe.)

The Apache knew their kinsmen by the language they spoke and the way they lived. How the Apache did things and what they believed was called the life-way.

There were differences between the Apache. Groups that lived in the desert shared many of the same beliefs, as did groups that lived in the plains.

Apache wickiups could be moved easily.

Most Apache lived in
small bands of five to ten
families. They shared work
and food. The bands
moved when the herds
moved or the seasons
changed.

This Apache family camped near Roosevelt Lake in Arizona about 1918.

Each band had four or more campgrounds where it lived for three to six months at a time. These camps were near water and were safe from surprise attacks.

APACHE WOMEN
AND MEN

Apache women built the
family huts called wickiups.
Women also gathered
twigs and brush to make

An abandoned wickiup

Apache *ramada*

their *ramada,* a shady
place for cooking, sewing,
and child care.

Women made the family
clothing. Animal skins were
used in early times. Later,
European cloth was used.

FLUTE

DECORATED POUCHES

CEREMONIAL DRUM
USED IN RITUAL DANCES

The pouches (left), flute (top), ceremonial drum (center),
and dolls (right) are examples of Apache craftsmanship and art.

Apache men were fighters.

They spent long hours making tools and weapons.

Apache men loved storytelling. It was their favorite pastime. They also enjoyed games of running.

13

APACHE MARRIAGE, LAWS, AND CUSTOMS

When a brave married, he went to live with his wife's band. He took care of his wife, her parents, and her younger sisters and brothers. A man could have two wives. But he had to be able to provide for both families.

Apache family (left). About 1890 this Apache family (right) was photographed bathing at Ojo Caliente, New Mexico.

There was little crime within the bands. An Apache who stole from his own group was a thief. A thief was made to give back the stolen goods and a bit more.

Anyone who killed a member of his or her band was taken to the victim's family. They passed sentence. Sometimes the sentence for murder was a beating; sometimes it was death. The worst punishment was being asked to leave the band. Living alone was unbearable for an Apache.

Geronimo (left, on horse) and Natchez (right, on horse) were famous Apache warriors.

APACHE LEADERS

Every band chose their own leader. He had to be strong. He could not brag.

A good leader listened to his people. He cared about them. He shared with them. No selfish person could ever be a leader.

At council meetings, local leaders sometimes chose a *nantan* as their spokesman. This is the closest thing to a tribal "chief" the Apache ever had. There never was a "chief" of all the Apache.

Apache
devil
dancers

RELIGIOUS BELIEFS AND SUPERSTITIONS

Ysun, the life-giver, was the Apache's god. Ysun sent the mountain spirits called Ganhs to teach the Apache how to live. Ysun also sent White Painted

Woman and Child of the Water to help them.

Every year all the Apache honored their spirits. They danced special dances and ate special foods.

The di-yins had charms and spells. These people could cure the sick or tell the future. They could give advice. There was a di-yin for everything in the life-way—marriage, birth, hunting, war, and much, much more.

Apache medicine man (left)
and a hunting charm (right)

No Apache would go
near a burial ground. They
were afraid of ghosts.

No Apache ever spoke
the names of the dead.
Their ghosts might appear!

Property belonging to a dead person was burned. Otherwise the dead might come back to get their belongings.

Owls and bears were believed to be forms used by ghosts to hurt people. So those animals were feared, too. An owl feather was thought to cause sickness and even death.

Cochise Peak (above) is in the Chiricahua Mountains (left) in Arizona.

The number four was lucky. Doing things four times was a part of their everyday life. The four directions—north, south, east, and west—were important to the Apache, too.

Apache women carried their babies in cradle boards.

GROWING UP APACHE

Children were important.
After birth, a baby was put
in a cradle board. The
mother carried the baby
for at least six months.

Geronimo's son and his wife (left). In 1892 Desar (right) was the Apache scout for the Tenth Cavalry.

In the spring of his first year, an Apache boy was given his first haircut. His hair was cut three more times. Then it was not cut again. Some braves let their hair grow to their waists.

25

Hoop game (above) played by the White River Apache in
1901. Before rifles Apache hunted with bows and arrows (below left).
They used them to fish in this 1885 photograph (below right).

26

The young Apache boy grew up listening to stories about hunting and raiding. Each boy knew that someday he would be a hunter and raider like his father and grandfathers.

Fathers made bows and arrows for their sons. The boys learned to hunt.

The boys grew older and stronger. Their fathers taught them more. Boys learned to run long distances. They were taught to use their senses—smell, touch, taste, sight, and hearing. Boys also learned how to move quickly but quietly.

As a boy neared his sixteenth birthday he was prepared for his manhood test. He had to go on four raids with the men of his group. If the boy did well on the four raids, he was called a man. He was free to marry, hunt, and raid with the men of his band.

He could even become a leader.

Apache girls were taught how to build the family's wickiup. They learned how to do things the Apache way.

At about age thirteen

Apache women learned to build wickiups and to make strong, colorful baskets.

The past and the present meet, as visitors watch a young girl take part in an Apache ceremony.

every Apache girl was given a four-day feast.

The girl was dressed in white. A wickiup was built for her so people could visit and bring gifts. During the four days the girl-woman was believed to

The Apache keep their ancient tribal traditions alive in today's world.

have the powers of the first mother on earth, White Painted Woman. She could give blessings and bring good luck to her people.

After the ceremony was over, she could marry. It was the most important event in a young girl's life.

GATHERING, HUNTING, AND RAIDING

The Apache got the things they needed in three ways: gathering, hunting, and raiding.

Women and children gathered food. Plants, fruits, and nuts were eaten.

A few bands grew corn, pumpkins, squash, melons, and chili peppers.

Apache on horseback (left) gather acorns in 1920. Corn (right) was an important food crop, too.

Every Apache male hunted. Deer was their favorite meat. The Apache hunted alone. First the Apache hunter greased his body with animal fat. This was done to cut the "human" smell.

The hunter put on a mask made from a deer's head. Then he waited.

When the hunter killed a deer, everybody ate. The meat was shared with the whole camp.

Some foods were not eaten. Prairie dogs, snakes, turkeys, and fish were believed to be unclean. Otters, badgers, and mountain lions were hunted only for their skins.

Bald eagle

Eagles were trapped and two or three feathers were plucked. Then the birds were set free.

Raiding was another form of hunting in the Apache mind. Settlers called it stealing, but the Apache didn't. To them it was necessary. They

Chiricahua Apache camp on the San Carlos River in Arizona about 1885.

raided ranches, small towns, and wagon trains regularly. They took what they could use.

Raiding parties were small—four to eight braves.

THE APACHE WARRIORS AND WARS

For nearly three hundred years the name Apache meant death to Spaniards, Mexicans, and all settlers.

As warriors the Apache gave no help to an enemy and asked for no help. They sometimes showed mercy to those who fought bravely, but cowards were killed in horrible ways.

Some of the greatest Apache warriors were

Mangas Coloradas (Red Sleeves), Cochise, Geronimo, and Victorio.

Apache warriors prepared themselves for battle. For four nights they did the "angry dance" (or war dance).

Mangas (left), Victorio (center), and Natchez, son of Cochise, were Apache warriors.

The warriors painted
their faces and chests with
the signs of war. They put
on war caps made of hide.
Then quietly they left
camp. Their families waited.

Apache warriors fought
to the death.

The Spaniards were the
first Europeans to explore
the Southwest. The Apache
began fighting them in the
1700s. When the Spaniards
left in 1824 the Mexicans
tried to defeat the Apache.
They lost.

In 1846 the Mexicans lost Texas, Arizona, and New Mexico to the United States. At first the Apache did not fight the American Pindah ("white-eyes").

Settlers came to the Southwest. The cowardly acts of a few people ended the peace. The leaders, Mangas and Cochise, fought the Pindah with a fury. But Mangas was killed.

Cochise knew that his people could not beat the

General Cook (second from left) met with Geronimo (third from left).

soldiers (Blue Coats).
There were too many of
them.

Cochise tried to end the
wars. Then Cochise died.
The Apache were told lies.
Promises were broken. At
last they were forced to

leave their lands. They were made to live on reservations. It was a bitter time.

Victorio and Geronimo were two Apache warriors. They tried reservation life, but their people were miserable. So Victorio and Geronimo led two separate groups away from the reservation. The Blue Coats hunted them down.

Victorio was killed in Mexico. Geronimo was captured on April 11, 1889.

About 1886 the Apache Indians, including Geronimo and Natchez, were sent under armed guard to Florida.

It took five thousand soldiers to force him to surrender. He was sent to Florida with many other Apache.

It was not until 1914 that the Apache were allowed to return to the Southwest to live.

THE APACHE TODAY

Today the Apache people live side by side with other Americans. Some Apache are farmers, others are cattle ranchers, journalists, filmmakers, teachers, and doctors.

The old ways are not gone. The Apache still do the dances and tell the stories of times past. But things have changed.

The Apache have a saying. For everything there

Apache lumbermen (top left),
mothers (left) and grandmothers
(above) live in the modern
world, but they keep
the old ways alive.

is a beginning. For all
things there is a reason for
being. When that reason is
over, there is an ending. . .
then a new beginning.

WORDS YOU SHOULD KNOW

band(BAND)—a group of people organized together for a purpose

belief(bee •LEAF)—something that is believed in, usually by a group of persons

brag(BRAG)—to talk about oneself boastfully

brave(BRAYV)—a warrior of an Indian tribe

ceremony(SAIR •uh •mo •nee)—a formal ritual performed in a serious, established manner

charm(CHARM)—something worn or carried that is thought to bring good luck

claim(KLAIM)—to take possession of, as the rightful owner

council(KAUN •sill)—a group of leaders representing those who elected or named them

coward(KAU •erd)—one who is afraid and has no courage

explore(ek •SPLOAR)—to search in order to discover something

gathering(GATH •uh •ring)—the collecting of plants to eat

independent(in •dee •PEN •dent)—not dependent; not under the control of others

kinsmen(KINZ •men)—relatives; people joined together by something in common

leader(LEED •er)—a person who leads or directs a group

mercy(MER •see)—compassion or help, given to someone who deserves punishment

miserable(MIZ •er •uh •bil)—unhappy; uncomfortable

newcomer(NOO •kuhm •er)—someone who has just arrived

pastime(PASS •tym)—something done to make the time pass pleasantly

punishment(PUN •ish •ment)—a penalty given to a person who has committed some kind of wrongdoing

raid(RAID)—to make a surprise attack on

reservation(rez •er •VAY •shun)—a plot of land set aside by a government for use by Indians

selfish(SELL •fish)—excessive concern for oneself, without thinking of others

sentence(SENT •unz)—the punishment for a crime, as given by a judge or court

spells(SPELLZ)—words which, when spoken, have the power of magic

spokesman(SPOHK •sman)—a person who speaks for others as their representative

thief(THEEF)—one who steals

tribe(TRYB)—a group of persons with something in common, such as race, ethnic background, blood relationship, etc.

unbearable(un •BAIR •uh •bil)—not bearable; too terrible to be endured

unclean(un •KLEEN)—impure and not usable because of moral or spiritual beliefs

warrior(WORE •yer)—a person whose main job is battle or warfare

INDEX

Americans, 37, 40-44

Anasazi Indians, 5

Apachu ("the enemy"), 6

Arizona, 5, 40

bands, family, 9, 10, 14-16, 17

bears, 22

Blue Coats (soldiers), 41, 42

boys, 25, 27, 28

Child of the Water, 20

children, 12, 24-31, 32

Chiricahua Indians, 7

clothing, 12

Cochise, 38, 40, 41

council meetings, 18

cradle boards, 24

crime, 15, 16

customs, 14-16

deer, 33, 34

di-yins, 20

Florida, 43

food, 32, 33, 34

four (lucky number), 23

Ganhs (mountain spirits), 19

gathering, 32

Geronimo, 38, 42

ghosts, 21

girls, 29-31

haircuts, braves', 25

Hohokam Indians, 5

Hopi Indians, 5

hunting, 33-35

Jicarilla Indians, 7

Kiowa-Apache Indians, 7

language, 8
laws, 14-16
leaders, 17, 18, 29
life-way, 8, 20
Lipan Indians, 7
lucky number, 23
Mangas Coloradas (Red
   Sleeves), 38, 40
manhood test, 28
marriage, 14, 28, 31
men, Apache, 13, 25, 27, 28, 33-36
Mescalero Indians, 7
Mexicans, 37, 39, 40
Mexico, 5, 42
nantan, 18
Navajo Indians, 7
New Mexico, 5, 40
owls, 22
Papago Indians, 5
Pindah ("white-eyes"), 40

Pueblo Indians, 5
raiding, 35, 36
ramada, 12
religious beliefs, 19-23
reservations, 42
running, 13, 27
Spaniards, 37, 39
storytelling, 13, 27
superstitions, 19-23
Texas, 6, 40
tribes, Apache, 7
Victorio, 38, 42
war dance ("angry dance"), 38
warriors, 37-43
Western Apache Indians, 7
White Painted Woman, 19-20, 31
wickiups, 11, 29, 30
women, Apache, 11, 12, 24, 32
Ysun (life-giver), 19
Zuni Indians, 5, 6

About the author

   Patricia C. McKissack and her husband, Fredrick, are freelance writers, editors, and teachers of writing. They are the owners and operators of All-Writing Services, located in Clayton, Missouri. Ms. McKissack, an award-winning editor, published author, and experienced educator, has taught writing at several St. Louis colleges and universities, including Lindenwood College, the University of Missouri at St. Louis, and Forest Park Community College.
   Since 1975, Ms. McKissack has published numerous magazine articles and stories for juvenile and adult readers. She has also conducted educational and editorial workshops throughout the country for a number of organizations, businesses, and universities.
   Patricia McKissack is the mother of three teenage sons. They all live in a large remodeled inner-city home in St. Louis. Aside from writing, which she considers a hobby as well as a career, Ms. McKissack likes to take care of her many plants.